Mapping Australia

Written by Richard Platt
Illustrated by Ludovic Sallé

Contents

Collins

The great South Land

How did we fail to notice Australia?
It's the size of Europe, yet Europeans
didn't spot it until the 17th century.

Of course, the vast land was no mystery
to Australia's Aboriginal people.
They'd lived there since sailing from
Asia more than 40,000 years ago.

It's not hard to see why white
explorers took so much longer to
find it. Australia wasn't on the way to
anywhere that Europeans wanted to go.

When they got there, European
explorers such as James Cook
did little more than nibble at
the edges. Their coast "maps"
were just bold outlines.

Mapping the middle was
an epic challenge. Many died exploring
the hot, dry **outback**. The picture
wasn't really complete until satellites
photographed Australia in the 1970s.

3

Songlines

Long before Europeans visited Australia, the people of the continent travelled great distances. They had maps to help them, but they weren't like the maps we know.

Instead, these Aboriginal or **indigenous** people found their way using songs, dances and religions.

Carved on rock

In a few places, ancient marks scratched and painted on rocks chart the land nearby. To indigenous people, these "maps" are **sacred**, and were created by the spirits who made the songlines.

They believed that spirits
from the past created
paths across the land
and sky. Travellers who
followed these songlines
or dreaming tracks could
avoid getting lost, hungry
or thirsty. The beat of
the songs and dances
helped them memorise
directions and landmarks.

Terra Australis

People from the top of the world imagined what was at the bottom long before they mapped or even saw it. 2,300 years ago they guessed there must be some great South Land, to "balance" the lands of Europe and Asia in the north.

Terra Australis fills the bottom of this 1604 map.

Greek thinker Aristotle was first to suggest Australia existed.

Five hundred years ago, mapmakers had begun to draw this imagined land, which some called *Terra Australis*, on world maps. They didn't know its shape, so they just guessed!

As **mariners** sailed farther and farther, they discovered new lands far to the south. But most of them turned out to be parts of Africa or South America. Perhaps the great southern continent didn't exist, after all?

First to land

The first European to visit Australia did so by mistake. In February 1606, Dutch mariner Willem Janszoon was exploring the coast of New Guinea. He sailed across the Arafura Sea by accident. He landed on the western side of Cape York, Australia's northern tip.

Janszoon met Aboriginal Australians and traded with them, but the mood soon turned angry. When Dutch sailors landed to collect food and water, the Australians attacked and killed several of them. Fearing more violence, Janszoon sailed away thinking he'd landed on the New Guinea coast.

the Dutch sailors firing at the Aboriginal Australians

Were the Portuguese first?

World maps drawn 50 years before Janszoon's voyage show what looks like Cape York. Some geographers think this proves that Portuguese mariners reached Australia before 1524.

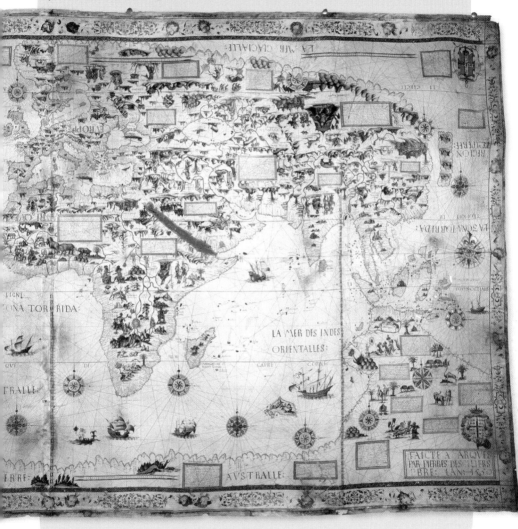

Dutch wrecks and maps

Dutch mariners began to sail a new route from 1611. Strong winds in the southern Indian Ocean blew them to their destination, Java, in half the usual time. Unfortunately, the same winds blew ships on to the west Australian coast.

Some were wrecked, but in 1616 Dirk Hartog landed at Shark Bay. He found the land **bleak** and boring, and stayed just two days, long enough to scratch details of his visit on a metal plate and leave it nailed to a post. As he sailed on to Java, Hartog mapped the Australian coast.

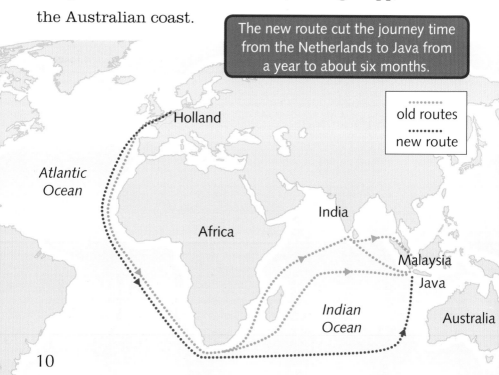

The new route cut the journey time from the Netherlands to Java from a year to about six months.

Holland

old routes
new route

Atlantic Ocean

India

Africa

Malaysia

Java

Indian Ocean

Australia

By 1627, the Dutch had maps of much of the west Australian coast, but they kept their discoveries a secret. They feared that other countries might claim the new land as their own.

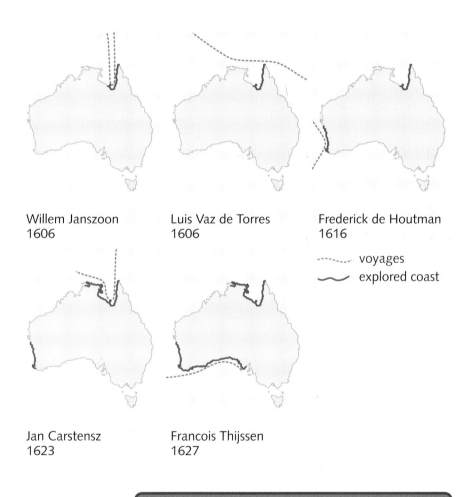

Willem Janszoon
1606

Luis Vaz de Torres
1606

Frederick de Houtman
1616

- - - - - - - voyages

~~~ explored coast

Jan Carstensz
1623

Francois Thijssen
1627

Dutch mariners explored the Australian coast little by little, gradually building up its outline.

11

Discovering New Holland

After these early discoveries, Dutch mariners went on to explore and map more of the Australian coast. Their aim was both to discover valuable new lands, and to chart rocks and shallows that might wreck ships. Thanks to the secrecy of the Dutch East India Company that they worked for, they had no competition. Many years would pass before sailors of other nations learnt about the vast continent, now called "New Holland".

Trading spices

The Dutch East India Company began in 1602 to bring valuable spices to Europe from Jakarta, Indonesia. The company grew hugely powerful, and stopped other nations from trading spices.

Dutch ships setting sail from Jakarta

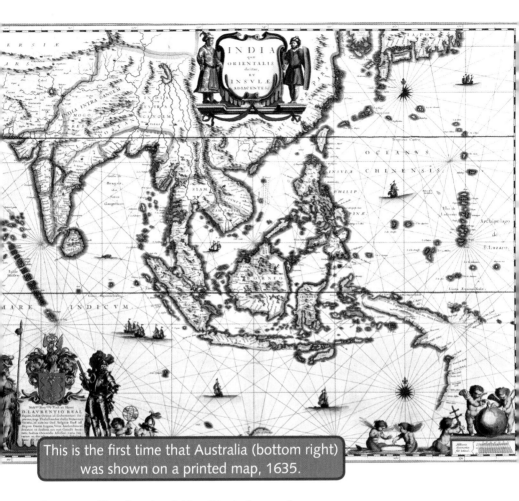

This is the first time that Australia (bottom right) was shown on a printed map, 1635.

Among the best of the Dutch explorers was Abel Tasman. In 1642–1643, he discovered New Zealand and Tasmania, which he named "Van Diemen's Land" after his boss. A year later, he mapped New Holland's north coast.

By 1659, Dutch mapmaker Joan Blaeu was able to draw most of the coast, except for the east.

13

Part 2: James Cook

Young James

A century after the Dutch discovered Australia, a young Englishman began to study sailing and mapmaking. His studies would later lead him to the great southern continent.

James Cook was born in 1728, in Yorkshire. He left school after just five years and worked on the family farm before getting a job in a grocer's shop in Staithes, a fishing port.

Living by the sea made him want to travel, and in 1746 James joined the crew of a coal ship. On its grimy decks, he learnt to sail, and he turned out to be very good at it. He was offered the command of a merchant ship, but then James did something nobody expected ...

To war!

To the amazement of his friends, James Cook joined the Royal Navy in 1755. The pay was bad, the food worse, and the work hard and dangerous. But James guessed that in the Navy he could command bigger, better ships. His captain soon spotted Cook's skills and, within a month, he gave James a more important job.

One of James's duties as part of his new job was to supervise the raising of the anchor.

Mapmaking and **navigation** need very similar skills.

Soon after Cook joined the Navy, Britain was at war. Cook's ship sailed for Canada and fought in battles against the French. Cook played a special part in British victories. By now a skilled mapmaker, he drew charts of the coasts. They showed safe channels for ships, and safe landing places for attacks.

For 150 years, there were no better maps of Newfoundland than Cook's.

Transit of Venus

In 1769, the planet Venus would pass between the Earth and the sun. Britain's most important scientific club, the Royal Society, wanted to send **astronomers** to Tahiti to watch this **rare** event. They chose James Cook to take them there.

Cook's ship, the Endeavour, arriving at Tahiti

18

After a seven-month voyage, Cook got ready for
the "transit", building a special **observatory** in a tent.
But the Earth's atmosphere blurred the shape of Venus.
Everyone was disappointed.

This wasn't the end of Cook's voyage. Observing Venus
was only half of his mission. His masters in the navy
had prepared another task, which they'd kept secret
even from Cook. Now he opened a sealed envelope to
read that he was to sail to *Terra Australis*!

Around New Zealand

Cook sailed his ship *Endeavour* south from Tahiti,
but found nothing. So he turned north again.
On 6 October 1769, a lookout shouted "Land ho!"
They'd reached New Zealand!

Going ashore for water, the sailors from *Endeavour*
met a group of native Maori people armed with spears.
Frightened, Cook ordered his men to open fire.
They killed several of the Maori. Many more would die
before the ship left New Zealand.

Cook didn't believe he'd reached *Terra Australis*, and he
proved it by sailing round the North and South Island.
On the way, he mapped the coast with amazing skill.

Plant hero

Joseph Banks was chief scientist on the voyage. The new kinds of plant and animal life he discovered made him famous.
Banks wasn't the first to see a kangaroo, but he gave the animal its name.

bottlebrush plant

mountain devil

scrub she-oak

king parrot

black petrel

red-tailed black cockatoo

Destination Oz

Endeavour sailed west, and after 20 days the crew spotted Australia's eastern shore. They were the first Europeans to see it. Sailing up the coast, Cook came to a huge **inlet**.

A group of Gweagal Australians watched as *Endeavour* anchored. Cook launched a boat to meet them. When two waved spears, Cook ordered his men to shoot, and the Australians fled.

When Cook got ashore, he took measurements of the land. Some earlier **surveys** measured distance roughly, using stretchy ropes, or by counting paces. Cook measured distances by using chains, which made his maps more accurate.

While the crew searched for food, wood and water, Joseph Banks collected plants and animals. There were so many that Cook named the spot Botany Bay.

Then they headed north again, mapping the coast, before sailing for home. They almost didn't make it. On the voyage north, a rock made a hole in *Endeavour* and the ship nearly sank.

Return and fame

When *Endeavour* reached England after nearly a year, its round-the-world voyage made sensational news. But the newspapers hardly mentioned Cook, for Joseph Banks grabbed all the **credit**. Journalists praised him and his collection of 3,000 plants and rocks. He became as famous as a modern pop star.

Glory came slower to Cook, for he was **modest**, claiming "I have made no great discoveries". Eventually though, the Navy gave him a better job, as commander, and he met the king. When another Pacific voyage was planned, Cook was chosen as leader.

New invention

While Cook was away, John Harrison made the first clock that worked on a ship. By measuring the time when the sun was highest, mariners could use it to judge how far they'd sailed east or west.

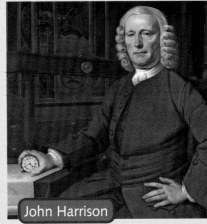

John Harrison

John Harrison's clock was called a chronometer.

Second time around

Despite Cook's discoveries, members of the Royal Society still believed that a great South Land might exist. Though Cook didn't agree, he sailed south to search for it in July 1772. This time the expedition had two ships – *Resolution* and *Adventure*.

This second voyage, which lasted three years, was another triumph for Cook. The two ships battled huge waves, fog and ice in the Southern Ocean.

The discoveries they made on their voyage proved that there was no great land at the bottom of the world. After exploring the South Pacific and discovering many more islands, Cook returned to England.

This time he was treated as a true hero, and Europe's greatest explorer.

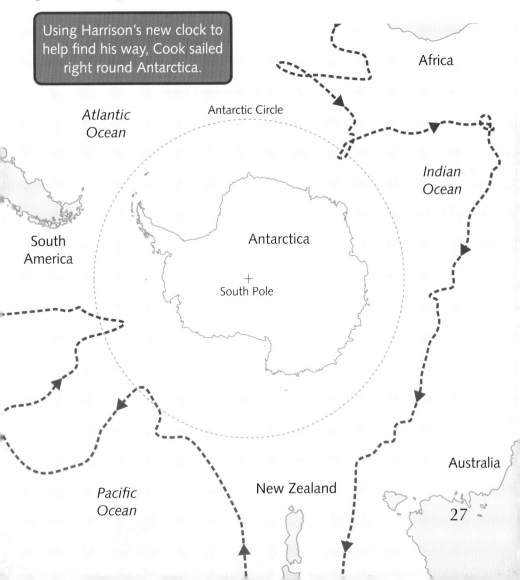

Using Harrison's new clock to help find his way, Cook sailed right round Antarctica.

Atlantic Ocean

Africa

Antarctic Circle

Indian Ocean

South America

Antarctica

+ South Pole

Australia

Pacific Ocean

New Zealand

The final voyage

Cook gave up sailing after his second voyage, but in 1776 the Navy tempted him back. They wanted him to search for the Northwest Passage. This sea route around the North Pole links the Pacific and Atlantic oceans. Cook set off in July and crossed the Pacific, discovering Hawaii. He continued east to map America's northwest coast.

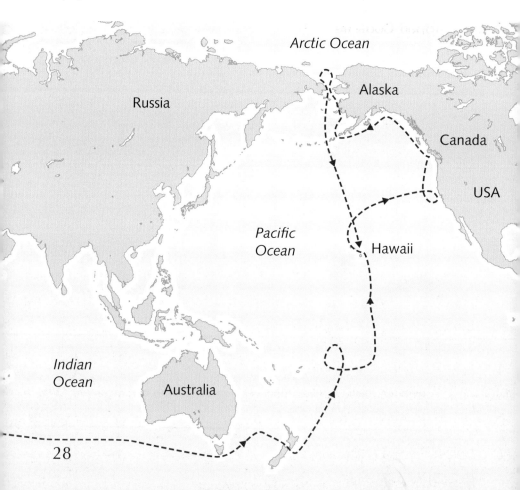

Discovery and *Resolution*
sailed on through
the Bering Strait between
Asia and America.
The frozen ocean stopped
them finding the passage
they were seeking, so they
sailed back to Hawaii.
There the people
worshipped Cook as
a god!

Cook was mistaken for
the god Lono because he
arrived at Hawaii during
a harvest festival.
Cook's diary brought the first
reports of surfing, which
the Hawaiians invented.

Death in Hawaii

The warm welcome didn't last. Cook's men were rude and violent, and didn't understand or respect local **customs**. By the time the ships left the island three weeks later, the Hawaiians were suspicious and angry.

The warriors wore "war-mats" as armour, which may have been made from coconut **fibre**. They stopped fearing guns after this armour stopped bullets.

The soldiers were reluctant to fight and badly trained. They didn't protect Cook, who'd become unpopular because of his **erratic** behaviour.

When storms damaged their ships' masts after
two days sailing, Cook returned to Hawaii. It was
a deadly mistake. The Hawaiians stole a boat from
their unwelcome guests. Cook tried to take their king
prisoner until it was returned. A battle began on
the beach, and armoured Hawaiian warriors killed Cook
and four soldiers.

Part 3: Completing the picture

Mapping the coast

James Cook's map
of the east coast
completed an outline
of the continent,
but there were still
details to fill in.

Early maps show
Tasmania joined on.

Nearly 20 years after
Cook's death in 1779,
English explorers
Matthew Flinders and
George Bass sailed
round Van Diemen's
Land, proving it was
an island.

Matthew Flinders

The Englishmen's voyage started a race to complete the map. Expeditions from France and England set off for Australia in 1801. Flinders commanded the British ship; Nicolas Baudin led the French expedition.

Their work took them two years. Making maps from their measurements took even longer. The first map of all of Australia's coast appeared in 1811.

An Aboriginal Australian called Bungaree helped Flinders survey the coast.

33

The river mystery

The first Australian maps were just outlines of the coast. What lay inland was a mystery. The biggest puzzle was in the southwest. Rivers there flowed west, away from the sea, but to where? Perhaps they poured into a huge lake? In 1829, English explorer Charles Sturt set off to find out.

His team launched a boat on the Murrumbidgee River and drifted downstream. They journeyed into other west-flowing rivers, into the Murray River, and then to the sea.

Now they had to row upstream, in the scorching Australian summer. Heat and hunger almost killed them, and Sturt went blind.

Sturt at the junction of the Murray and Darling river, 1830.

Charles Sturt at
the Murray river, 1836

But the mission proved that there was no inland sea,
and they mapped a little more of the vast continent.

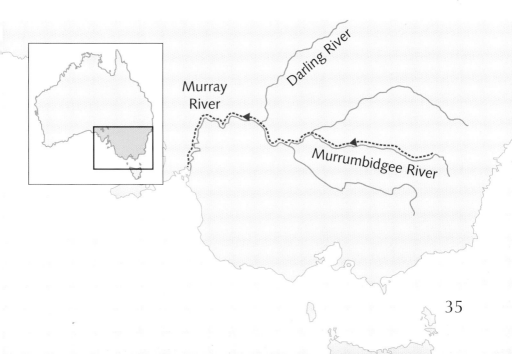

Murray
River

Darling River

Murrumbidgee River

Filling in the middle

Discovering Australia's wild **interior** took most of the 19th century. Many brave explorers set out from the coast, and not all returned alive.

An Englishman called Edward Eyre travelled from west to east in 1840. An Aboriginal guide called Wylie helped him survive the desert trek without shade or water.

Starving Eyre ate his horse and learnt from Wylie to drink dew from a bark cup.

German scientist Ludwig Leichhardt crossed the continent's northeast corner in 1844. Praised as a hero, he later vanished on a trek from east to west coasts.

In 1860, British explorers Robert Burke and William Wills set off from Melbourne, aiming to reach the north coast, 3,250 kilometres away. Their badly-planned expedition took far too much equipment. Though they crossed the continent, seven men died, including the leaders.

Ludwig Leichhardt

Burke and Wills brought over 24 camels from India and six more were bought from a zoo.

Forgotten heroes

The footprints of **pioneering** explorers left tracks across Australia's outline, but it took a long time to fill in the rest. Surveys only began when European settlers needed maps of their farms and building plots.

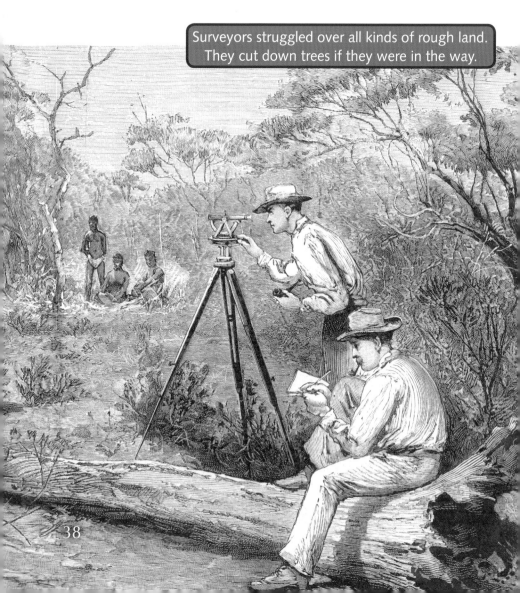

Surveyors struggled over all kinds of rough land. They cut down trees if they were in the way.

Surveyors using chains to measure distances.

To draw the boundaries, an army of **surveyors** set out from Australia's coastal cities. With chains and survey instruments on tripods (three-legged stands) they braved intense heat, hunger and insects.

Each state had its own surveyors, and the maps they made weren't accurate. Merging maps at state borders proved impossible.

Mapping of the whole continent had to wait until World War Two. The Australian army wanted maps to fight a Japanese invasion that never came.

Eye in the sky

Mapping Australia was slow because the outback was huge, hot and **remote**. But in the early 20th century, mapmakers found a new, quicker way to work. They fixed cameras to newly-invented aeroplanes, and made maps from photographs. The first air surveys of Australia began in the 1920s. After World War Two ended in 1945, the Royal Australian Airforce flew missions over the continent. Their overlapping pictures recorded heights as well as distances.

The Royal Australian Airforce's 87 Squadron pioneered air surveys.

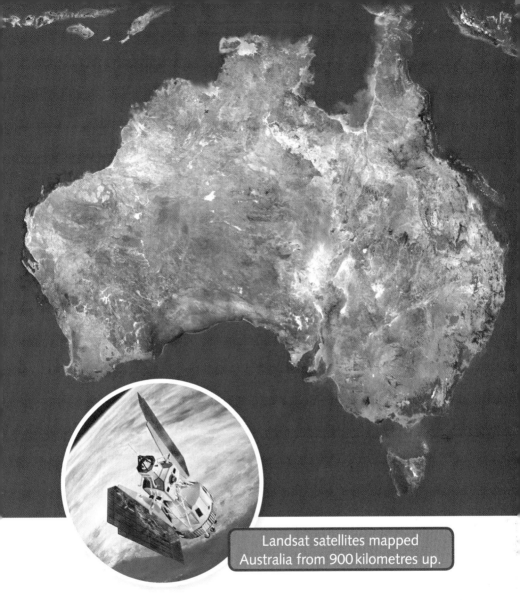

Landsat satellites mapped
Australia from 900 kilometres up.

In the 1960s, cameras on satellites took the first
pictures from space. Within ten years, the pictures were
good enough for mapmaking. By 1980, satellites had
mapped all of Australia.

Whose land is it anyway?

A map is a useful tool for finding your way around a strange place, but it's much more than this. To own land and to sell it, you first need to map it. By mapping Australia, European settlers claimed the continent as their own.

However, the land wasn't theirs. Aboriginal Australians had lived there for 45,000 years before Europeans arrived.

Britain used Australia as a vast prison, but after prisoners had finished their sentences they were given free land to farm.

In the 1940s, Aboriginal Australians began to protest
about the way white Australians treated them.
They wanted their stolen lands back.

Laws changed slowly, but by 1975 half of the Northern
Territory had been given back to its indigenous people.
Other states have also returned land. At last
Australia's maps are changing again, putting right
a 400-year-old **injustice**.

Glossary

astronomers   scientists who study the stars

bleak   empty and without shelter

credit   praise and glory

customs   the usual ways of behaving

erratic   unexpected and odd

fibre   hair from a plant or animal

indigenous   original or first

injustice   something unfair

inlet   part of the shore where the sea has cut a small channel into the land

interior   land away from the coast

mariners   sailors and others who go to sea in ships

modest   not proud, and unwilling to claim glory

navigation   finding the way using maps

observatory   place for looking at the stars and sky

outback   the countryside, away from the cities

pioneering   using new methods

rare   not usually found

remote   distant from other places

sacred   respected and honoured, especially for religious reasons

surveyors   people who map the land

surveys   measurements of the land to make maps

Index

Explorers and mapmakers

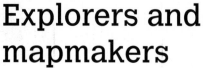

1769/1772
James Cook lands in Australia

Since 45,000 BCE
Aboriginal indigenous people of Australia

1500   **1600**   **1700**

1616
Dirk Hartog lands at Shark Bay

1524
Portuguese mariners

1829
Charles Sturt

1860
Robert Burke and
William Wills

1840
Edward Eyre and Wylie

1800

1900

2000

1844
Ludwig Leichhardt

1960s
Landsat 3
satellite

1779
Matthew Flinders
and George Bass

1945
Royal Australian Airforce

Ideas for reading

Written by Clare Dowdall, PhD
Lecturer and Primary Literacy Consultant

Reading objectives:
- retrieve and record information from non-fiction
- discuss their understanding and explain the meaning of words in context
- identify main ideas drawn from more than one paragraph and summarise ideas

Spoken language objectives:
- participate in discussions, presentations, performances, role play, improvisations and debates

Curriculum links: Geography – locational knowledge; geographical skills

Resources: globe or map of the world, ICT, drawing materials.

Build a context for reading

- Ask if anyone has been to Australia and discuss what is known about Australia, e.g. Where is it? What's it like there? Find Australia on a map or globe.
- Look carefully at the front cover and discuss the pictures. Ask children to suggest what is happening in the illustrations (measuring and mapping).
- Read the blurb together. Focus on the title Mapping Australia. Help children understand that places are "mapped" in different ways by different groups who live and visit there.

Understand and apply reading strategies

- Read pp2–5 together. Ask children to recount some key facts and make sense of them, e.g. Australia was first noticed by Europeans 300 years ago; satellites were needed to map the interior.